T0147508

TREK OF THE

◆

CHESHIRE

A, masterful, journey, into, the, aquadrant, times, of, author, Lark Voorhies. An, elective, abbreviate, that, casts, trace, above, known, entitlements, 'pon, astloe, monuments, to, date.

Lark Voorhies

iUniverse, Inc.
Bloomington

Trek of the Cheshire
A, masterful, journey, into, the, aquadrant, times, of, author,
Lark Voorhies. An, elective, abbreviate, that, casts, trace, above,
known, entitlements, 'pon, astloe, monuments, to, date.

Copyright © 2011 Lark Voorhies

iUniverse books may be ordered through booksellers or by contacting:

iUniverse
1663 Liberty Drive
Bloomington, IN 47403
www.iuniverse.com
1-800-Authors (1-800-288-4677)

ISBN: 978-1-4620-2598-5 (sc)
ISBN: 978-1-4620-2599-2 (e)

Printed in the United States of America

iUniverse rev. date: 6/9/2011

PLUTO ARISING!

◆

I will, always, breakdown my environment, to its, basic, components, and, recreate a reality all my own. I will, always, breakdown my environment, to its, basic, components, and, re-create a reality all my own. I will, always, breakdown my environment, to its, basic, components, and, do whatever it is, in the will, or, world, I want to!

With that, I, set, in, to, cleanse, and, reclaim, sanctuary. For, surely, t'is in this space, where, I spend so much of my time in renewal. Bring my thoughts in for examination, speak my riddles into solution, daring to be what I brave to think: that I can construct initiation within the productive fortification, and, respect for personal barrier. I believe this is why I have always felt safe here, in process of bathe, and, groom. Acknowledging the present, bringing forth the new. All, the work of inspiration, backed with improvisation, as my spirit dictates its most recent design. Where, no one rules, but, my own. Always, and, Amen. I cradle in the thought.

I take moment to beam at my strangeness. Reclining on the lid seat, in the guest suite of my great aunt's home, content, within the 6'1/2" by 12' enclosure of adobe wall, and, Euro-antique design. Complete, with personal, exotic effects all my own.

Resting, foot-top of the counter, whose cabinets, both, simple, and, ornate, find themselves wrapped within the same, pink, uniformity expressed by the walls, served notice, by the light carpet, and, the bright, expansive ceiling. The mirrors, wrap around pronouncing corners, flanking the central window. Trimmed in crisp, white linen, and lace, it speaks in whispers, as it both diffuses, and, magnifies all available light.

1

I squint to keep her secrets. Taking in ancient pose as she locks offer in tarrahs, unspoken. Keepsakes for those who'd be kin of mine.

T'is, within, this, acquaintance, that, I, profound. Home is where the heart is, indeed.

SENSATION.

◆

Wince. At the many trips I took before my fall. On category in particular, sensation. And, my fight to win it back from within, the depths of my inner hell.

I was dormant. Reduced to square inches of my soul. I could feel nothing within, and, nothing without. So, I went searching. For sensation.

Bumping, and, bruising my outer membrane, so that the shockwaves could penetrate to stimulate growth through, to, within the little of me that was left. And the lie. Ah, the, lie. T'was, only, my path through solid wall. A menial means to an old end.

The body count is, (sigh),overwhelming in retrospect. Friends... loves...a path that I must constantly groom on my pilgrimage to center. I motion, in veil of my dignity. Opting to say that the day I closed the door to humiliation's love, is the day I set out to confirm by my own will. Any way I dared. Cheshire.

There were some sweet moments. The rest, just, fuselage. Deleted files. Cleared for the, better, purpose. Thank God for awakenings.

A return to friends...I haven't met a, real, one, yet. As, it stands, now, I, esteem, my house. Yes, it, gets stripped, and, cleansed, once, in, every, new, season.

Friends, are labyrinths of awelcomed ritual. So far, I've, only, seemed to find my way into mazes. Backing up, and out with much, regretful attitude. Now, I just pick them up, I, examine their little games, and, wind, up, finger-polting them, right back into their, little, toy, box. Case closed.

On the subject of loves...haven't yet met a restful fusion on the cabeza tip. Most memorable were the emotional connections. The rest, defined, carnal waste. No, slacking, for me. I live this life, and, I have no time for the excuse.

Accredit to the emotional connections, are, the, moments, of, pure, gesture. For, they are what kept me warm in a cold reality. T'is to these places, I go, for reflection, and, rest. T'is to these places, I have always been able to unwind, and, nest. T'is to these places, I owe the construction of "me".

That's the miracle of the human spirit. All are but a time machine with the execution of your will, and, sight of advancement.

Sweet spaces of sweeter sensation. Each building a layer to the surface. I go back as often as I can.

Cheshire.

WHO YOU TALKIN' TO?

◆

Tick-tock, and, time to flex.

Everyone's got a season of postulate. A little shadowboxing of sorts. Especially women! Me? Well, I cat, mice, and, screw you into a comma, that's, what. Cheshire.

March 25th, 1974. Pisian-Aries-Tiger…what?

From the beginning. (Ahem) What is a cusp? If you were born within the first, or, last five days of an anualogical, sign, then you are relative, to two sun signs. Creating a very uncommon, and, interesting mixture. Again, my primary, Aries, is ruled by Mars. My influence, Pisces, is relegated by Pluto. Now, my moon is in Taurus, and, ruled by Venus. As, I was born in the year of the Chinese Tiger…don't bother. Here's the breakdown:

Aries: never lacks for excitement. Full-blooded, independent, forceful female. Accept it, or, leave. Wants to be understood, and, appreciated. An irresistible force of reckoning. Most certainly ambitious. Your staunchest ally. Will fight side by side with you, believe in you, encourage you. No man becomes her Lord, and, Master. Meets her man on equal terms. She is no pebble, nor is she a sourpuss. Mirrors what she receive, either by initiation, or, response.

Mars: Planet of aggression, and, of physical energy. Governs sex drive, and, forcefulness. Red colored, fiery planet. Name means "Bright, and, Burning one". The Roman God of war. Exalted in battle, and, strife. Never hesitating before leaping into the fray. Governs energy, boldness, the will to win. Hates to be ordered around. Strong leader. Adventurous, pioneering. Quick-tempered, brash impulsive, and, impatient. Planet of passion.

Pisces: Planet of earthly passion, and, unearthly fantasies. Cannot plumb the depths of the enticing allure. Mysterious way of uncovering the secrets that lie beneath the social mask, through to real motives. Sensitive to the slightest nuance. Greatest need is to unite in an almost mystic communion. Completely adaptable, woman of a thousand faces. Remains completely, and, uniquely, herself. Elusive, untouchable, mysterious. Daydreams are truest reality.

Pluto: Planet of awesome power. Still found, largely, inexplicable, and, difficult to understand. Brings light to the things hidden in your subconscious. Releases your dormant forces, causing your suppressed energies to suddenly erupt. Originally called planet X. Now, named after the Roman God of the underworld. Signifies death, and, rebirth. Nuclear fission both destroys, and, creates. The highest, and, lowest of which man is capable.

Taurus: Da Vinci, in the art of seduction, with her Mona Lisa smile, yet, not at all promiscuous. Any, hopeful, male, picking up her seductive signal, had better turn off his antenna if all he wants is a casual affair. Or, risk the wrath of her affliction. A natural earth mother, she loves, and, nurtures, giving of her strength. Having a secure sense of her own judgments, and, needs. Trusts her own instincts. Being in love brings out the best in her, though she is never really won. Makes up her own mind. Plans ahead. Never lets you know you ever had a choice. Cheshire.

Venus: Planet of love, and of pleasure. Dominion is love, and, the emotions, power of the heart. Steals the wits of even the wise. Temperamental, indulgent, treacherous, and, spiteful, governing the higher emotions. Her gift is of happiness, making life beautiful. Travels far from the sun.

Tiger: Charming, persuasive. Can talk anyone into following. Tenacious. Bounces back quickly from set-backs, or, adversity. Arrogance is a weakness. Boredom is a weakness. Does not listen to fools. Uses foresight before forging ahead into the horizon.

Aries Tiger: Impatient, head strong, creative. Restless, sexy, and, knowledgeable. A double Aries. A double tiger. Outspoken, blunt, and, sensuous. Fiery, passionate, a troubleshooter. Generously loving, and, kind. Very, very bad tempered if crossed.

Pisces Tiger: An unusual combination. Ruthless efficiency, and, determination with sensitivity, and, emotional release. Likes to express emotionally, and, dramatically, yet are soft, and, warm. Hard, and, muscular mentally, yet are emotionally fluid, and, beautiful.

In so many words, by this book's closing, this is what you will have come to discover, as, I balance my planets, and, shadow box, on time, in time: the, need, to, examine, more closely, your own intentions, thoughts, and, formats. The why, how, and, ought to do's that, lead, to, the, quality, and, annality, of your life.

This has been me. God, knows, its, good, for a dutiful, pep-talk, any day!

HOW TO CATCH AN ECHO.

◆

How do you go, seamlessly, from the object of oblivion, to one of, complete, intrigue? From profound misunderstanding, to one of V.I.P., private invitation? From violent outburst, to one of absolute retraction? All in one night. While still managing to be, wholly, everything twilst, yourself? Why, you catch an echo. And, unite. Until it becomes one.

The night I discovered this formula, was the night, I knew, it could be no other way.

I'd spent 24 years, living in the model of personal opinion. The past three, developing a model all my own. Following all of the basic, time-honored, framework. Fleshing it out in ways that would, be, only, uniquely, "me".

Being, that I took on a masculine roll within the household of my, single, family, parentage, I suppose it was only a matter of time before my training, my, developing, preferences, shaped by the pace of a, changing, world, came colliding. Joy.

That year was 1998. The year I separated, in marriage, for the first time.

Ah. My, the segue from spring to summer, and , the foreshadowing to my final take off!

Newly elected, first, African-American, spokes-model for a major, hair campaign, I saw this as prime opportunity for the reinvention of my life.

Wanting to begin such a daunting task, on that high note, I announced my decision. Searched for, and, found a place beyond the, hometown, city, limits still claiming me. I sat up in complete silence, again, for the first time, really, ever. I was elated, and, terrified, and, alone. The echoes were back. (sigh) But this time, I was ready for the challenge.

Bravely, in paper, & plastic bags, I, hurriedly, packed away, most of my life, for the move, and, change. As they covered the, newly, occupied, living room floor, of my new, one-bedroom, apartment, I, knew, this, would, be, a, true, rocket, of, events, set, for, current. In, representation, of, any way, that I could get away (with it!), I, occupied, an air mattress for a bed, and, little to no other furnishings. This was the scene of my new beginning. From, stone, scratch. Voila! And, toute, aplinge`.

Today, I would follow that "statement" with a sporting, "Ah. Just how I like it!" Cheshire.

Yet, I wasn't so brave then. And, My Thelma & Louise hurriedly shrank into the grace under fire. Fear, and, inexperience became the all too regretted reconciliation. Darn!

So, we tried again. So, we did. Only for me to leave everything behind, and, start, again. From scratch.

This time, I delegate to my echoes. For all, intended, purposes, if they were going to be around, they might as well be good for something. Right? Truly, apost all due declare. I tell you, pushing me around any further was, no, longer, an, issue, reuse. For sure! For certain! Prompt, post! And, on vow! Cheshire.

TO THE SURFACE.

What a breakthrough we had this day! Mighty lion, learned, new trick.

My, Grandfather, born on the first quarter of the 20th Century. Product of the World War, and of Great depression. Young eyes to the Decade of Decadence, and, all traditional fortitude, therein. A staunch, "My way, or, the highway," patriot.

"Me." Born, in the final quarter of, operative, civil rights, and, feminist, movements. Fresh eyes to the generation of excess. Pilot to the future! Warrior princess to the throne!

Grandmother's tension was not enough to tame the roar of wills this time. Along with my, flexing, tempest, I want him to know my love. A woman, is his granddaughter, now. A woman, with a mind, and, a will all her own. That will survive this translation of his.

How, peculiar, this space of quiet, determined, rage must be to his, nearly, 84 years. His, jewel blue, pillars, suspended between captivated awe, and, whoop-ass! He's still got it in him to do it, too!

Before I, fully, accept this, I close my argument, once he is fully expressed, and, breeze off, on, into my wing. Swollen with justification, and, uncertainty. "That's it!" He calls off, after me. "I'll leave then!" I snort. Rounding the corner, and, spilling into my bathroom, to inspect my newest reflection. "Wow!" "What was that?"

Recessing into the kitchen, then, hours after the gravity of restoration, Mom's wisdom. I cross paths with the great cat, once again. Silent, signals, are answered, and, received.

A slice of, homemade, cake, and, a glass of wine, later. Friends, again. Cheshire.

PAUSE.

A name is better than good oil. – Ecclesiastes 9:1

Rapt in attention, as my grandmother relays her memory of my first, spoken, word. A major event, coming from a family that rests its pride, primarily, on intellectual achievement. An extraordinary, visua, of a moment, in that my firstborn right(s) would be characterized, carved out, and, defined by this impromptu phonetic. And, a monumental outaking, in that, there would be no recapitulation. This, amazing phenomena, would be my, introductory. Debut. My, som-iterary, say. The peak of my encoded prestige. With no pressure from the surround of universe, I perceive, and, acquiesce my cue. Partitioning the, ceaseless, yet, mortal fibers, I take stage. Meting out my boundary, I prepare my expose'. Sensing my chart, on course, I hone the key, sharpen utensil, and, pronounce my truest entry. My, known, name.

It all began when, mom, decided to incorporate an exercise instituted by dad. This was, to stand over my attention, gleam into my eyes, and, whistle. He would do this, while snapping his fingers. Mom, noticed how I would echo every detail of express. How, I'd hover in the beam of his focal point for as long as he was willing. Pursing, and, manipulating, first, and, third digits to acquire perfect immolation. Blood of his blood, my father found his, first, loyal, audience within the purest form of my, thus, worshipful, respect. And, as my intense, little face told of the exertion it took to harness all, available, motor skills in order to achieve this effect, my, mother, on, alert, got the notion to take the, song, and, dance one step further.

One day, she began phonetically pronounce, in one syllable. L-a-r-k. Same, hovered, position. One, determined, soul. Beams locked in place. Raption, on target. After a repetition of 3, for, she never conceived such immediate turnaround, I answered, clear as a bell, from my primary diaphragm…"Laaaaaaark."

The whole house, consisting of just my mother, was in an uproar.

Ring-ring! Ring-ring! The grapevine was in operative, and, my premier note, in full swing. Verdict in, I will always remember who I am through the rotation of repetition to each, and, every relative near, and, far.

I was 5-months old.

Thus developed the ,healthy, practice of inward mastery. Achieveing, any, and, all, newly, introduced data. Previous to its outward composition. Thank you, father. Thank you, mother.

PAUSE.

I sit here, penning through the night. Peering through the doubled-doors of my room.

Beyond the manicured trees, over the leisure brickway, and, around the, Roman, fountain to catch the, sudden, royal, blue hue of the once dark expanse. I hear a bird, sound off in attention to the new day. And, it occurs to me. A, Lark, I am, indeed.

"What's in a name?" Asked Juliette. Most oft, more than a name is credited for.

For they are, to me, prophecy, and, mini-scripture. An etch of path defining, both, your future endeavor, and, the, succeeded reality. A name, literally, has, in its context, the power to ignite, in comportment, the, millenialed, trek of your horizon. T'is the opening, and, closing to what is regarded in relation to you, yourself. That, along with tonation, and, response, can be found, illicit educate within, the, very pronounce. Quite the prelude to majesty. I'll say. Cheshire.

In my yester-years, I wasn't quite at ease with where it took me. Not, quite, masculine. Hardly, feminine. Yet, center to a stage of world tradition, and, category.

Amazingly enough, I did grow, into my proper name. Wasn't too keen on its, exotic, inflection. Yet, once, inside of a mature space, I found its treasure; the obligatory gift to reach, messenger, move, achieve, and, declare. It's a wonderful instrument. Strong in articulation. Commanding, crisp. Enunciation of its power, from the, introduced, dominant consonant, to the last. Catching the attention, and, fulfilling its prose. Mate.

I am, indeed, a Lark.

THANK YOU, MRS. CYRUS.

$\blacklozenge$

Honestly, and, from the foundation of my heart of hearts. For you, both, began, and, polished off my world of education. T'was you, who awakened the sleeping giant. Insighting the insatiable hunger of a, determinately, wise, and, infinitely, curious mind. T'was you, who championed to challenge my every notion, coaching me to levels of escalate. T'was you, who went beyond description to stimulate, and, encouraged the fruition of any, and, all accessible capacity. And, just, as you aligned strategy to my lesson plan, enhancing surfacing skills, t'was you, who brought me in touch to whom I really, could, be, and, to, whom, I, really am. And, I thank you.

"Heart of hearts. We'll start there." She determined, early, one morning.

How pitiful I must have looked to her, as my shifting expressions gave me away. "Where, exactly, is that?" I supposed, gathering myself up, from unstbetween that, mental obstruction. Mrs. Cyrus, just sort of propping herself. Studying me. I didn't know the answer. So, I squirmed, and, writhed in spirit, and, form trying to figure this sacred philosophy. And, it angered me that, at 16, I was so out of touch with the experience of "how I 'felt.'"

She awakened the importance of knowing "why." Not just existing in place, but, finding purpose within the position. T'was she, who thought better to fibrillate the dormant fight. T'was she, who charged my inner champion to strive to the peak of courage. T'was she, who set me on the finer courses of intellect, and, literacy. T'was she. T'was she. T'was she.

Thank you.

PAUSE.

Ah. To the topic of boys. You know, those things you come across, that cause your heart, and, mind to dosey-doe. Make everything around you grow hot, and, silent, and, cause complete loss of sensation from the hip-joint, down? Yes, those things. Oh, the wonderful trouble they cause.

Fortunately, and, unfortunately, they, had, graced my intermissions amongst growth, for as long as I could remember. And, I, had, discovered, the, two, basic, categories, ladies, and, gentlemen: the Power Horse, and, the Bad, Boy. Oh, for whatever the category, the two, forseemed, to remain, a, non-interchangeable. Proceed.

The Power Horse: a real one, a rare find. And, lack the charm, and, charisma it takes to stay afloat, a Bad Boy. Tending toward the pretty face, to mold, and, tame, and, own, they miss the blessing of reality agrown. Though they do, naturally understand the world, its exchange, and, its resourced payoff, a life of fancy free, doesn't become, to, them, without the natural, standoff, honest, and, deed. A, far truth.

The bad boy, though so endowed, lack the wit, and, know how it takes to script even single notes in the symphony of, the true, operative levels of reality. Though, the mystery they spin, does make for a wonderful world of fantastic, visceral travel. They're likely to allow you passage, and, examination to their tangled web, if you return it sensible, and, improved. Earning their trust is quite a strategy. The world is yours, if you make it. Ruling it together is how they like it. A life of whallery.

Wherever, you coin it. However, you spin it, the world of men, is not one easily done without. Choose wisely. Proof.

Cheshire.

PAUSE.

Question:

Why, is it, that if, you are not demure, and, are able to speak to a man, while looking him square in the face, let, alone, the eye (generally what they expect, and, ask for), does he find the need, therefore, translate it as fair to call to your desire, thereor, proceed to call you outside of your name?

Why, when it's clear, that I ace, crown, check, and, mate you, yet allow myself to settle for equal, you, cue that as threat to title, bout, and ownership?

Why, when the time comes (and, it does), for me to claim what is clearly mine (and, I do), do you, smokescreen with, such, indiscrete word? The term, in truth, is lioness. Get it right! Glint.

Cheshire.

SENSATION.

Warning: not for the faint of heart. For, these are memoires of sensation. Ahem...Proceeding.

And, we begin...

"Oh...wait...oh, my God...what is this? What...is...happening...to... my...body? Is...this...what...it's supposed ...to ...do?"

I am frozen. And, in light. Awakened, by my first, female awareness. And, I'm seeing in panoramic.

I sit here, at the foot of my bed, loomed in the midst of this memory. With the only available light flowing from my bathroom chandeliers. Joe Sample, and, Lela Hathaway play on my, silver, boom-box, of, clear, plumbed, accents. Surrounded by scripts, notebooks, novels, and, candles.

I tell you, where physical stimulation failed me, there was always the cerebral.

As, I am, comforted, by the perfume of my, rose, incent, I give thanks for sensation.

Most of my only, lonely, childhood was experienced within this vaccum. A fortified membrane, that only the purest, and, most, honest waves of, fluid, music could victor to penetrate.

Each note, on trial, as it attempted to woo me, into love.

Music: The, adept, tenuation. Directional to modes of cheer, and gender.

Music: An, oration, of, trusts. Clear huened, to, an, oranthropy, of design, and, splendor.

Music: The, only, absolute, singular, thing that ever, really, touched this only, lonely child.

Pluto, you are, as well, a good friend, indeed.

On, global, scales. I take in the world, around me, through the world around me. Savoring every shade. Every tone. Every stunt. Every stone. In that way, any, and, everything I'll ever want, I can claim, as, any, and, everything I'll ever need. Already owned.

I, thank God, for language, and, the varied arts of communication. I, thank God, for his wisdom, whence training my, selective, membrane. For, shining upon me, in the dark. Keying me in to this gift, this constant of sensation. This, entirely, indelible thing. And, really, I just find myself, thanking God.

SENSATION.

(Sigh) How, I remember that leg of my life, so well.

That, profound, time, and, space, discovered in adolescence, where you are the center, and, focused attention of any, and, all of your prerogatives. Styling on, for size. Factoring, figuring. Refining, definitions of what would be. Loved it.

My, buffufled, order needed grooming, however. Immediately.

Summer, 1988. 14, and in the final leg of the strangest, though, most, helpful, years of my, educate, and, career. 8th grade. In one of the, finest, yet, tiniest parochial schools to ever exist.

A class of, child, prodigies, passing through, on their way to build time's, encompassed, oblivion.

The love of diction, and, literature did swell there, along with an abbreviated course on how to use our individual, as well as, collective muscle to insight change in an open world, through the effective execution of properly invested skill, and, the focus of special capacity. Thereby, profiting your, well placed contribution. Exciting for us all.

Be it, "The Grapes of Wrath," "of Mice, and, Men," "The Pearl," or, "Travels with Charlie," John Steinbeck, easily became one of my favorite authors, save his ability to make his experience yours. "Macbeth," and, "Romeo & Juliette," covered Shakespeare, "Death of a Salesman," and, "Les Miserables," the tragedies.

So, I had a heaven away, and, a heaven familiar, as I'd engage my social life well into the twilight. Conversations, comparisons, arrivals. Only, to spin the rotation into the dawn. Carpe` Di`em!

TO THE SURFACE.

♦

Syperbia! Being hyper-sensitive to the subtext of, human, nature. Nothing like it. Packs a punch, and adds spice to your, greeting, and, meeting, agenda for the day. If you know what I'm punching at?

Can, also, be a drain to your spirit, if you don't posses your own arena's worth of, self-sustaining, comprise. Why be vulnerable, when you can self-mote. Reencompass your ticket's worth?

Never mind the spite, the malice, the mind-game attempt. Most people will hate, because, it is the most familiar sensation. Familiar, is not proverbial. They hate, because, they are afraid of themselves. And, are afraid of themselves, because, you are not. Tragedy.

Try laughing. Heartily. Examining the chips, labeling old adages. Sighting the steaks, and, raising them plenty. Ta ta.

So, "Into the dragon's lair, I go. Emerging with new friend, old foe." T'is my life's mantra. The trick is in the getting away, should you come across an specially cross one. Like, the hero. I, always, manage a getaway. With, the girl, the statute, and, the varies of splendor. One must survive the perilous highs. Once, one has conquered the treacherous, and, impending, lows. Wink.

Win, I say! Say it with me. I will win! It's mathematical, it's probable. It has the source of any means necessary.

Adue.

SENSATION.

◆

On my off hours, I too was battling the, awkward, torment of adolescence. That, swelling, and, insecure, uncertainty. The, constant, trying on for size...the, always in question...that, never, quite sure. Enough. Ahhgggg!

I hated everything. And, was certain, everyone else did too. Glad I retired that head.

At that time, I hadn't made form of the blurs. And, awonder, whatn't they had done with me. And, so, I stood, thereby, alone, in the eye of the storm.

An already complex circumstance, about to advance, to the mark, in the awakening of my young adulthood. There hadn't a better time for prayer.

Stimulation of the mind, through wrote, and, music, would soon be joined by the natural, court, in simulation. Candor! Everybody. Candor!

And, so, there I was, on my way, becoming a woman. Shiver. More victories won whereont that sea of loss. How, grateful. I believed in something greater. To stand in the wash of my early fall. Those times that I lay there, lethargic, aching in sorrow. Waves, lapping at me. Ground, leaving me. "If, I don't get up, the hungry swells will surely reclaim me." For sure. Move!

The journey, to find, and, collect the elements that would give life-saving meaning to the unmotivated. Unmovable. The strength it would take, to muster auxiliary care. The willingness, to yield to better know-how. The wisdom, to graze, and, glean your aware. These are the things life has come to enlighten to me. Though, stoneworthy, the path of the one who finds that, they are the unmotivated, themselves.

So, you see, there are two ways to go about rising up. There is the path of the turbulent adolescent, disturbing your balance, and, sense of well being, during the day, along with the, young, delinquent, class that rob you of your youth at night. Or, you can mode above standard.

You can start, by listening to that which you should. Which is not always that which you want. It hurts to apply. It's worse to fail. Your choice. Beware, the false tides. Cheshire.

WELCOME, TO MY SOUL.

With the growth of the physical body, there comes an awakening. In the growth of the mind, there is profound undertaking. Growth of the emotions is absurd, unpredictable, painful, even. Much like extracting a, highly, regenerative, stroke of virus from your chest cavity.

This, I understand, well. Major stretches of life spent steeping within the occupation of this sensitive membrane. There, I could seize upon territory. There, I could challenge explore.

By stopping up your ears, you can establish that, which I mean. The, plugged, vaccum. For, t'is there, in which, I , in fact, dwelt.

T'is in this place, I am found vulnerable. T'is in this place, I lay out all defense against that which would be infectious data. T'is in the place, I found quest to run.

To terms!

WELCOME, TO MY SOUL.

◆

It begins, a, pinpoint, knotting of glowing heat. Dead center, searing to sternum. The wave of volt, triggers an alert. Thoughts turn inward, and, against, as vines of self awareness fill my frame. The suspicious growth leaves me one, lone, eye through which to perceive reality.

Finally. The explosive will to live, slices through all congestion. Clearing the way to free. Relieving my speech of its razored adornments. Increasing in white air.

In the ethereal stillness of post-storm weather, the tempest evaporates. Leaving, only, electric, beauty. A qualient, clearing, for true beginning.

Signing on. Amen.

WELCOME, TO MY SOUL.

♦

Train people to expect nothing, and, the least, little, thing gets them all excited.

Ask Pavlov.

And, so goes the, hyper-vicive, philosophy of my personal/professional enterprise. The, tragic, beauty of belief systems. Tuning in for that dose of irony, in a wafer-thin world does wonders for a, sharding, sense of humor, dulled by the elements.

Such a, precious, energy is only relative to the agreements you make. Where something is wrong with everything, information is opt, most, relevant. Agreed.

Now, if, in toll, truth, will, indeed, set free. How, franchising, the world of realists, and, starvebound, the globe of materialists. Truth.

Looking back, all of my, personal, torment can be surmised by the, very real, encompassment of missed cues. Telling engagements, of multitudinous grace, mixed format, ascued delivery. There is nothing that has evented my life, that I didn't, see, first. And, dispense, respectively. Nothing, that didn't harbor the pitch of planning. Yet, everything, foreknown, was, always, indicted. Always, circumnound. And, ever, present for measure.

Point being: Yes, I've, omitted, nonsense, that, to my credit, I should have spotted, and, cared for, immediately. Yes, I wish to equiess all, accountable, avenues programmed, and, designed for my success. Yes, I wish to practice concern, where perfect sense is available. And, yes, I wish to, hyprophilize, my placement, exchange, and greet. Securing Scholar's fame. Tightening the night.

Only, if I charge the way, will I see the eventide. And, only, if I serve the fight, will I take, flight, air. Only, if I mean the plight, will I press coast Ogleby. And, only, if I sight the night, will I shame the hornbey.

Sweet Night.

WELCOME, TO MY SOUL.

◆

Wealth: the, active, imbursement, distribution, and, or, reckoning of one's residual means of staple.

Investment. What most will call grace, or, giving. A, mere, down payment, to entitlement toward the object of such generosity. Is a pharse. A facade, a veneer, in promotion of the prominent, though unworthy .

Alien to this concept, in regard, the surrounding expanse, keenly aware to this, one-sided, gift of the lush. Where, the pulse of the minority doesn't equate to their, minor acts.

One, grows weary, tired, even, of balancing the trites. The, hungry, energy of careless souls. Preferring the company of, the solitary, productive. The world translates sad state, when, personal gain, becomes hailed above all else. And, the plights of the known, are the things resurgent.

In minuet, with that inescapable truth, time, has nurtured, and, engineered a stay-hard bridge, and, an official crossing to reciprocity.

In the knowledge of this, I awake, some nights, and, mornings, chest fluttering, in the revamp, of this generational synopsis. Knowing, the, abbreviated, stanza will recess symphone, without quality interjection. There is a need, a, required, status, due to the plummeting resources, vs., rising demand. In that, delicate, geometric, promotion is this, soloist. Featured, protected, displined. Entries, are prized. Well guarded. Fulfilling these roles, is a, necessary, evil, to the gaining of satiation, and, view. For, only, the privileged access the truer silation. Fortunately, or, not, this is so.

What will prove in the predestination?

WELCOME, TO MY SOUL.

♦

The, majority, of human, consensus, in the realm of interrelation, I have found to be, shallow. Void, to non-existent. For, the, reband, and, reconcile, assuage, through summation, and, compartmentalization. Effectively, and, on the regular. In, upstanding, dosages, this is critical. However, parted to dissemblance, the vehicle transpires the effectate of plague, and, procession. Pity.

There seems to be, for to the above described, an innate sense to fear. Spoken earlier.

At will, they dehumanize, in dissection, of what they can neither manage, influence, or, control. In, full, prestige, they occlude. Raising the mark, beyond all, markable, achievement, and, entitlement.

The system, has been expressed, I say. To its credit, there has been little more than marginal advancement. It serves me to say, success has been irrelevant. For, served it has not. When, the majority of mankind has been forced into the dissidence through which they finance their decadence, it t'is a shame. In all the whiled expressions, they have conclude, to a stale, statutory, not. Full, of the confines of enrelishment. Quite. Quite. Enough.

Cheshire.

ART & LITERATURE.

◆

Discerningly, t'is, only, as, edificiary, for me to establish the reality of my own, natural, life, as it is for others to distinguish, from its fantastic affair. For, I work within a cosmetic industry. However, my method, and, manner, neither resplances, nor, evades. But, rather, it intrigues, or, throws.

Allow me to explain.

You see, the, constant, measure, and, review, from, both worlds, clues me into, exclusive, retreat, on quite the regular. Here, I am endowed to write, read, catch up, if you will, on the world through music, and, media. Here, I explore all of the, very, personal, things that collect, and, bring me to center. Here, again, I establish my, own, critique, philander my own party. Sort, and, design the idiom of world. Where, I express, and, choice. Manifest through application, and, establish the, well nourished. Where, I have challenge to call friend, and, life, proports, otherwise, to call me. For, he always tells me the truth, expects the best, and, cheers it out of me every step of the way.

Improved, I return to the world current. Championing my, newest, collect against the past, and, present atone. Invigorated reviews, and, charmed eloquence, grace this, fortuitous, encounter. Melding, and, applying, to a polite peak. And, the cycle begins, again.

Now, in these spaces, one does find the very nature of one's self not always to be so splendid. So, when there, seemed, incurable facets to the lonely. Oh, there were, multitudes, of applicable innodes. However, none quite like art & literature.

Why, music invoked well with the silence. And, the incumberment of read, satisfied all, intellectual, stimulous, required, to ingratiate, and, bless the, elemental, starve-cried soul. With spirit complete, motivation proved to be the luxury. For, you hadn't but to be, and, the material spelled its magic, anyway. Encouraged, cheered back from the abyss, it gave its all, to you. All of you. Every time. In an unpredictable world, this was the constant I could stand.

Where, music, would be the preference, and, my love. I would play whatever I could get my hands on. Whatever, my soul called for. Knowing, every piece, by accent, and, heart. Oh, the, reese, hollow.

Cheshire.

Contentedly: infused, I emerge unto scene. Ready, to cheer the world, again.

Halelu. Corvestu. Enter, continue. Harvest, and, truth.

I go back, as, often as I can. Cheshire.

THANK YOU, MRS. CYRUS.

◆

It, charges me to say, in onus, in order to better, edify, this, MVP, Scholar on, information, and, motherhood, that you are, indeed, my, championed, Plymouth. My, usher of orb, my, erstwhile, glimmer. For it was she, who, first, took to measuring, and, formally, instilling the, time-honored, vestibules that would carry me through my prodigious, scholarly, career. Counting me worthy of the investment. Thank you.

This, richly, steeped, tea-brown, woman, with dusted freckles, unyielding, supply of bangles, and, two, low-positioned braids, twisted into design, at the base of her great mind, was the premier to the explore of the Pluto in mine.

To understand, any further, you must, first, appreciate the, position, homogeneous. And, the, rogue, import of the faction of my life.

There was, and, still this is true, none like her. Out of all of the people within my, young, experience, there was, no one, as mystical, enigmatic as Mrs. Cyrus. For, she was truly, other worldly.

Oft times, I would aconcience myself in gaze at her. In, determine, to decode. Obdurate, upon unlocking her mystery.

There was that, amongst an arsenal of other musical stimulous, that held you to her cadence. That, she used well. An, ethereal, utopian, of heaven, and, earth, as translated, and, filtered through her powerful ability to speak, bite size. Astonishing, the way she maintained the intrinsic from her bag of distraction, for her introvenal feed.

I remember, class, being, one, long, game of cat, and, mouse. As, we bounced, from one station of, delirious, fun, to the next. It, was divine, as I never tired of each, new thing.

Upon meeting with her, again, 10 years later, in studio-school, it, t'was a pleasure, I hadn't anticipated. Perhaps to say that I had mixed emotions is more appropriate. Wink.

On the one hand, I was rather excited to have the opportunity to build with her, again, and, at this level. On the other, I knew she was here to regulate. (Sigh). My days of, indulgent, getting by were over.

Wrapping my mind around this, scholastic, boot-camp, that I was sure that, what she had attruncted to her person, was an, astoundingly, unpropitious wrench to my, wonted, routine. For, a young lady, who was treading water on a, sleepy, set school, I, suppose, I should have been grateful to the agenda. For it was to mean my benefit. To a young lady, accustomed to negotiating high marks, while multitasking to the tempo of the Discman, this was a, startling, invasion to my, founded, establishment. My cozy domicile, had been interrupted, and, who knew what was in that case she now shuttled in, like a B.R.A.T. patrolman. I tell you, it was Dr. Sues vs. green eggs, and, ham, and, I wasn't a taker. (Height). Sigh. A new sheriff in town. Tide, and, woe.

THANK YOU, MRS. CYRUS.

◆

"That to which much is given, much will be expected." -

I remember her smile. That measured look. As, she, scrolled through her cranial files, confirming all, effective, avenues through which to remold my neglected state. Then, ZAP! BAM! BOOM! We were, again, in wonderland. I was Alice, and this Cheshire had me cornered.

She was relentless. Yet, up building. She saw potential, and, on her post, she would not stop. T'was your will, against hers. Rev-rev-rev… Go! Okay, I'm in.

We swept over the basics, mildly challenging, to, effectively, astute. All of this, in quest of the local to my academic coordinates. Then, she piled on the curriculum. Meow.

My, two, years with her were constructive masochism. I'd found that magic, again. The method to her madness…learning. In, one, year, this woman, took from Spanish 3, clear through to 5. From, Algebra I to Calculus. She brought history, and, chemistry alive for me. And, the world became more than a dull routine.

She triggered the consideration to stop, second-guessing, myself. Reminding me of my intelligence. "Be confident." She would always say. "It will show."

Serving, as, both counselor, and, defender, she, helped, toole, my, hard-packed soil, into the garden. Blooming award-winning daisies.

Thank God for teachers! All of them, all of their forms. For, without them, we do, indeed, remain in wasteful slumber. Cheshire.

PAUSE.

It is often, I have wondered, "Did I really take the life of my family, with the breath of my own?"

Could that, blast, upon them, instigated by my birth, have, really, affected so much devastation? Could it have been, so massive a lesson, on balance, and, priority? A lesson on action vs. calculation? That unconditional, is not without obligation? Loyalty, without proof?

These, and, other truths, have been depicted throughout the constant processi, within the filing of my mind. Directly effected, I discretion concern for the breakdown of our, carefully, constructed set up. There was happiness, at one time. I remember feeling it. Comparing, and, matching it to the other fragments I saved. (Pause).

"Why." Both, my antagonist, and, hero.

He can sure go. These days, so can I.

Until, he gives me what the smell-a-fancy, I came for. "I," "Make my day, punk." Cheshire.

They're, not heavy. They're, my family. They're, not heavy.

They're, my family. They're, not heavy. They're, my family.

TO THE SURFACE.

◆

In the night, checkout time, for most, I am pure, and, protected. Waking, from my sleep with, answers, to the concerns about my day. Responding, with confidence to the challenge of Fear's, ridden, riddles. Another layer of my core, recruited. Solid. Good, and without pretention.

Question: Why, when, there, portune feavorish, beliefs, awence, the prose, of, maturation, do, ideals, play out sour, amongst, trailing, brites, where, halls, dim, in, fliency? Do, the, wonders, afloat, krale, atide, to mote, fallen timbers, quest, known, chides, at, member, when, neither, is true?

I believe, what most women want, is, indeed, an, amicable, forbearance, in partnership with professionalism, and a long run, within, available, chapmanship. True? True. Cheshire.

Question: Why should, introspection, be judged, measured, or, classified by those, who clearly, are, only, able to perceive, little, station, or, audience with, even, introversion? Is the, perspective, art of silence so terrifying? I suppose, the X, Y, Z, unknown, in relation, is always demonized. (Sigh)

Statement: As I am, so fulfilled in my station of self-accountability. I'm secured, the position of, asset, is, indeed, all it's cracked up to be. Not, trying to petition for permission from the tradition to be myself. Nor, am I trying to become awarded by diverting the cost, equivalent. However, wouldn't the, primary, expense be, first, afforded, then rewarded? On, what level, do you come to play?

Statement: Laughing at the fact, that habits don't change, they just get old. Starting, for the 3rd time, from ground-zero, I've appreciated the education, and, the build. In, truth, fear, is never the loss. Master the risk. Be present. Enjoy the ride. Love the conquest. I do. As, I possess the bookmarks to resource at will. I aim, flex, and, fire, in the game of conquest. Planning ahead, marking my scores. Always, claiming my bounty. Real McCoy, thoroughly enforced. Cheers!

TO THE SURFACE.

I rest my head, within the pinch of my nasal-brow. Elbow, in the care of my other hand. Which, rests, in the fold of my lap. Trying to wrap my mind around the, very, complex situation. If. Why? And, how? To place myself in a 72-hour watch. Imagine that. How, I got myself to this bridge, is just as much a mystery to me. Say, would you mind, spotting, me that map again? Cheshire.

Well, now. All of those thoughts you're having? I've had them, already. Several times over. Sitting, in that spot, alone.

Yet, what do you do, with, an, unexpected, turn of a frame of mind that, until, now, has so easily abyssed your demons? They've learned to swim, and, can, now, reach me, at will. A 25-year old escape route, closed off. Without notice. I pout, in grimace. "Hmm…"

Trapped, I am. Panicked. And, searching for air. Fighting my way through. Fighting my way for. Fighting, my, way, out… A, place which was, once, safe, is no longer. Hmm. How will I do this?

Ears, reach to listen, as negotiations are being made, and, protocol, followed, in lou of my present condition.

The reports upon my declining state are, indeed, a bit, too grave to bear. My body releases, in disappointment. As, even I am not found convinced in today's, "I'm okay."

Sweating in the reality that I have become, unpredictable, in thoust, personal, pain. Even, to myself. I sigh a whimper. And, glare through the blur of angry defeat. "Alright, I'll just go!" I blurt out. Not, believing, I had just said that.

My one concern: Will I be a match for my demons on dry land?

TO THE SURFACE..

$\blacklozenge$

I, retrospect, would do it all again. For this experience, in its entire, has proven to me, beyond a shadow of a doubt, that there...is...nothing... wrong...with...me. Sigh, and, Amen. Cheshire.

Confirmed, within the core of my being. No doubt. Whatsoever. Scene.

What I learned is that people have profound hurt, and, or fears that they neither know how to address, nor, answer for. They are, caught up, in a whim, and haven't a soul to care, or, give attention to. They, in essence, get bullied, by themselves.

That revelation, was, at first, absurd to me. If, it took wrestling this heifer, to a strait, so that I could engage, and, think, likewise, well. That's-a-what-a-I was-a-going to do. Bum-pum!

"Bring it, or shut it!" was my mantra, during these, dry, land, battles. Effective to this day! Cheshire.

Durring the three-days, I became, very, Dr. Spock-ish. Little, to no emotion at all. Only, the logical, and, the illogical. For, if you don't become, mentally, armored, your emotions will buy into just about anything, now, won't they? And, they pour it on. These, mental, Olympics. Onward. Charge!

So, there, I sit. In the examination chair of one of the emergency suites. Being questioned by the under aged, overworked, routine, that's penning, and, padding it before me. "Who, is she talking to?" I keep translating through, emotionless, gaze. "I may apreen, in youth, however, I am a, grown, woman. You nimcumpoop!

Making forms of the blur, I could hardly believe that this was the front line of the establishment. "Kindly, give me the forms, and, instructions, so, that I can get this on with. Kay?" For, I tell you, if I had to instruct her on how to help me, we were in for a golden one, if you know what I'm saying?

No, I wasn't the, highlighted, portion of her textbook. Nor did, I need, thwarted, cum bai ya, hold your hand, special attention. I simply, needed this to be a study of how I got here, and, how to get out. Having my thesis, finishing line be on, how, never ever to come back. You see?

So, there I am. Moments later, being wheelied. Down, hallways. Through, corridors. Stabilizing my overnight bag, on my lap, and, against my chest. Eyes, focused on the unseen. Still, with thought. Peculiar, as to what should be felt about these last, few, moments. About the person I, presently, am. And, as I probe, deeper, into this place, where, surely, everyone will be speaking to me as if I've just learned English, and, have to translate to me in rooky-speak. I am aware, that I must stand up to my intellectual level, or be doomed the length of, clinical, toddler-toot. In all of this, I do wonder, "What will remain through the fire?"

My attention, catches, as a wrong turn is taken, and, I'm pushed through the double doors of the living dead. My eye adjusts from the light of the hallway, to scan the coordinates of this dark end.

The, only, light, appears from this brain-dulling illumination of, centralized infusion. Why, the room looks like it's glowing in the dark.

Two rows of, closed, doors (tiny windows, included), as far as you can see, flanking either side of the main station for operations, and, staff. Yes, Lobotomy 101. (Purse)

"You've got to be kidding, me." I start up with, exacting, seriousness. "I'm not staying in this place!" I coach, while the escort races for the front desk, in order to confirm my declaration. "Sorry, about that." He surrender on his hyped-skip walk back. "Wrong turn."

As, I've lost my appetite to chew patuti, I return to my thoughts. Save, I spend the action, to match that, horrid, mistake. Truly. Cheshire.

Ahh. New set of double doors, better scene. At least, it's well lit anyway.

They, check me in, and, scan my belongings. Making sure, I don't have any objects that would harm the, average, child. (sigh) This sure had better turn out to be a massive improvement on anything I could have done on my own. I tell you!

They see me to my, sleeping, chemical. I crawl into, one, of two beds that I have, to myself, tonight.

"Do not tell any of this to my family!" Are my, strict, orders, as, my, trusted, alliance, spent, and, masking, deep, concern, peels himself away. Retracing his hone to the car. Then, to our home. Alone.

My math, twinkling, at me through, patches, of, charcoal, haze, and, black, night, sky.

Adue.

TO THE SURFACE.

You know (and, most should agree), I've never corresponded with the idea of waiting to be saved. For, I've always needed to know I could save, myself, if help wasn't around. Even, in the vissage.

Far from the cutesy, cuddly-type. Not alikening to being stroked, and, admired. I've never, exchanged my dignity for my identity. Never.

The faction of me that got along, to run, and hide, away, within my great escape, exists no longer. It has never sensed well with me. And, never mind about the things it has said about me to my very face. (Humph) Or the way it aches for resolution. (Humph) For finish. Cheshire.

I couldn't just stop at the victory over my dryland wake. For, being well aware, made me wholly accountable. I was not going to repeat that rotation of those, past, 25 years.

No more, hiding out form the elements. For tide does bring me to shore. No more, of the gnawing at my square peg. For, it finds its place quite nicely. No more, understudy, quandaries. For, time has fired the mold, and, impressed me to lead.

In all of this, adventure, I need to secure beyond the shadows, that I will prevail, on my own. (Meow)

PAUSE.

◆

Matching eyes of rage to hold, or, make a point is an art that you either master, or fail, sink, or swim, root, or, wither in one, solid sitting.

One does memoir these triumphant cells of achievement. Archives of tenacious and, acquired reward, seized, and, maintained epitaphs filed, and, coded, for archopological application, and, finesse, build, and, gridded accelerate.

When, one proceeds according to this outline, one may achieve, attain, even, the outstanding, at conceived proportions, and, realized will. A healthy start to any, if not most, or all, perceivable, pinochets, or, elitist rounds. Ole!

No, the serum to, legitimate, mate` is not in the trousseaux, or truffled meanderings of the textiled play. T'is in the unwind of each, and, every, mastered, foresight, and, stratagem. You must hold under the development of your accessible progenerate.

These, infinitesimal innuendoes are an all, too, necessary minuet. Relay, is a perspective dance.

Now, how does one score an honest win according to the design, advance, and, scheduled arrival of the goal at hand? Question: do you qualify to the design, and, or mastery of the desired quantum? Is the measured ratio proportionate to your ability to magnify, and, or materialize the genius of the opportunity? Do you rate high in, or, ascertain power of coordinate? Enough to gate, or, bull through to conquest, victory?

The footwork for this training field, more than all, other, places, should, and, most, oft, begins at youth. Truly. I've proportioned this life to have more to do with the natural prowess, than the array of dissemblance one airs to the practicing world. Par example: and, I remember these moments well. The intense study, the threatening snorts, the closing gap of two faces. In those moments, who will bend? Who will prove swift? Greater in artillery? How is the patrician gained? In those moments, you will discover who you are. I remember, wondering if a punch would be thrown? Would I feel it? Could I beat him? We were so young. My love kept fists from those rounds. Those stand offs I, still, close, with horn to, bigger, enrelishments. When the heat surfaced, and, we had, with chorus, had enough.

As with reality, there are few moments of trial, and, error, and, more held by what is at the heart of your skin.

If, the eyes are the window to all that is to be accessed, and, the most endowed gain the victory, then, be prepared to account for all you dictate. Literally. Cheshire.

TO THE SURFACE.

◆

I remember the first, and, only, time I met my father's Father. My grandfather. From whom I get my shading, eyes, basic, form, and, quiet intense.

At, 3, I, remember, boarding the plane, in mother's best. My, dainty, velvet, rose, pant suit. White, laced, collar, and, cuff. Matching barrette. White, patent, leather shoes. Frou-frou, socks. Entering, this, new, plan, walking down the isle, I remember the world of identical meticulousness. Rows, and, rows of same. Most, possibly, to imply, safety, and, order. Wink.

Traveling, in the air, was an experience, I remember, I rather enjoyed. There were, the, big, rubber, and, plastic earphones, the, really, nice, lady, who always brought, more, 7-up, and, peanuts, and, the movies. As, much as you could stand, high, on the monitor, just above my junior strain.

I, remember, the pressure, that would, build, in my ear. As, I, yawned my way off to sleep. I remember being in that, giant, seat. Mom, awakening me, as, that, nice lady, greeted me, with an official, airline pin. Clutching my wings, I scoot, past the rows, up the ramp, and into my grandmother's strong arms. Who, always, hugs me just enough. Her, coiled affection, overwhelming me.

I, remember, grandmother, laughing, a lot. And, reminding, me, of Mrs. Butterworth. The syrup, she buys for me, at the market. Along with the ginger bread cookies, she, buys for my cousin Robbie, and, myself.

My family is quiet, but, they do know how to keep company. As we play the commercial against the gingerbread men. Nook, table, in the kitchen.

The, very distinct, accent, I remember about, her, is the, laughter. Grandma, seemed, to laugh at, everything, while, nothing, laughed at her. Why, she's, probably, laughing, now. Cheshire.

T'was, a, cool, gauge, as, a child, in my lifetime. A life of musical chairs. Where you knew you were safe, as, long, as, long as the music kept playing. When it stopped, you could sense there was trouble, and, hoped that t'wasn't you.

Grandfather, was a bit of, always, quiet, and, to, himself. Always, reserved, gentle, and, smiled, when he looked at me. Very, very, stern, when he wasn't. A very serious man. Didn't talk, much. Yet, I know, he, likes, me. Because, he, grants, me, entrance, into, his room. Just sort of allows me to glance, and, look around. Silently, I ask, and, am granted permission to explore, each, and, the, next, item.

This is my , only, memory, of my, Father's, Dad.

TO THE SURFACE.

◆

Post-war, sensibility. Technological, incubation, of indulgence. The, bridge, to gap. The threads of relation become vintaged, and, rare. No, longer made by the manufacturers. New millennium tailors, study the seam. Calculate the blend.

traditions, of gender. Traditions, of thought. Traditions, of function, and, execution. All, arranged, and, operating. All pillars, and, routine. All, rhythms, and, materials, passing through the same wall, fired to consideration. Worthy study, to our age of advancement. Humored by fear of change, we are paced, yet, steady. Determined. In time, with love. Fueled, with hope. Steady, in the balance of truth.

The movement, is, unmoteable. Yet, are we ready?

Cheshire.

TO THE SURFACE.

◆

Conversation, after, conversation. Same, dull, wrestle, of, communicative, thought. Yours, to mine. Cheshire.

That was my, constant, frustration with adolescence. Watching the loop, as, I, stroll through the hole.

With a roll, of, my eye. Laughing at the thought. The notion. Having Thoughts, and, purposes of my, own. Am, I, not, interesting?

I'll own, difficult, and, complex, right along, with, brilliant, funny, honest, and, loyal. Soft, as, butter, tough, as, nails. The whole nine. Yet, I will fail to tolerate the cancel out of my exist, and, present, by way of your two points on my word game. You're, near sighted, and, still, don't see me? Cheshire.

I remember being the leader, into what was defined, as, "trouble." Well, at least I was the leader. Wink.

I, remember, there was time, and, again, with my, inspirationally-driven, cousins. Defying everything. Mastering the finer point of getting away, scott-free.

There was, the triumphing to the top of the roof, to , close in on this guy, Santa's, viewpoint on the world. Incomplete without a proverbial peek down that chimney. Then, showing my cousins, how I could delight, and, amaze them, complete, with whole books of matches. Commanding, the hunt down, and, flare up of each one we could find. Early scientists, according to my schedule, and, prediction. Simply, not, keen, to the major fact that scent travels. Cheshire. Yet, active in the gathering, of, whole piles of leafs, books of match, and, lighter fluid. A beautiful theme!

With me, delegating, constructing, and, composing, all the way. The, entire, show! Step right up!

Yes! Tree, equal, parts, to, one, amazing, bon-fire! Right, smack, dead center, to the front yard. Shine! No, laboratory, what could I say? Good thing, recompense is swift, and, leisurely. Aye?

If neither physical assault, nor, material depravity could stop me before, why should it ever?

A tackle is a tackle. And, fare is square. Don't whine "foul", just because I'm a girl. Or, otherwise, outside of your, comfort zone. Go, bench yourself! Angst!

TO THE SURFACE.

♦

I, remember, a, time, when, I, was, inclined, to, expression, with, everyone, in, regard, to the, details, detrimental, to, inner, torment. How, I, was, dancing. Smiling, to, the, beat. Behuve, my, heart, there, surfaced, afleet, to, hide, and, weep.

Charm, and, altogether, manner, belied, an, incredible, decompositional, sorrow. I, wondered, in, my, peculiar, state, quite, most of the time. Why, dealing, in, life, seemed, so, much, easier, for, everyone, in regard to the attention for clamor.

Now, case, in, point: conversation, wasn't, far, from, interview. An, ongoing, revel, of what, why, and, how? What, is, this, torrid, melancholy? How, do , you, best, prevail? Why, do, these, conditions, exist, within, contrarily, higher, decibels? Finally, how, the, smell-a-fancy, does, one, remove, this, screaming, cavity, from, my, chestplate? I, wanted, out, of, this, immobilizing, emotion.

So, I, did, for, a, while, somehow. Conversations, began, to, open, up, along, the lines, of, the, Trojan score. The victor vs. the champion. I, took, full, opportunity, to, find, cleansing, in, the, release. Thankful, for, the, catalyst, listening, ear.

I, had, been told, for, so, long, that, I must, have, misunderstood, what was, indeed, happening, to, me. That, I, didn't, know, what, I, was, talking, about. I, chose, to believe these things, in order, to, keep, from, having, to, contemplate, the, alone, concepts, that, were, just, a, wee, bit, over, my, sophistication, and, grasp.

When, I, began, to, coordinate, and, come, to, terms, with , the, ugly, truth, there, was, no, turning, back. I didn't, understand, why, how, or, for, however, long, it, was, going, to, take, to, leverage, this issue. But, the, war, was, on! An, alarm, had, gone, off, somewhere, and, I, had, no, choice, but, to, come, out, swinging. Smirk. Grin. Boom!

I, tell, you. For, 19, years, I, was, a, harborer, of, other, people's, dark, secrets. Then, one, day, the, question, arose. Why, be, good, to, them, at, the, expense, of, my, well, being? The, journey, began, with, one, conversation.

Natural, or, acquired, silence, is, criminal, to, those, who, require, vindication, through, testimony. 9, years, into, the, victory, I, still, am, able, to, comprise, the, gain, of, meaning. 9, years, into, the, victory, I, am, terrified, and, inspired, as, I, build, again, onst, once, upon, a, time. 9, years, into the write, I, am, finally, arrived, at, "me."

T'is, this, celebration, I, chose, to, verify, throughout, the, selection, of, this, book. Not, the, sordid, details. Yet, a, spotlight, on, testimony. In, contribution, to, the, movement, on, the, flood, issue, of, self-accountability. Now, a, wisdom, of, experience, through, my, storehouse, of, wisdom, and, peace.

For, comfort, o , your, denial, shall, never, be, exchanged, for, the, rape, of, my, innocence. You, should, never, be, able, to, live, with, that, EVER!

T'is, language, that, makes, me, free.

T'is, language, I, use, to supplement the, void, of, meaningful, speech.

For, it, t'is, in, language, there, lies, an, answer, to, reality.

I, had, to, be, present. My, life, was, calling; I, had, to, manifest.

I, gain, inspiration, from, the, figures. Managing, to, live, through, unencumbered, moldings.

To, life, forces, that, beat, the, odds...CHEER!

Cheshire.

TO THE SURFACE.

Thinking, upon, it. I, cannot, confess, to, surrendering, to, control, of, any, sort. I, can, only, say, that , I, tolerated, the, theatrical, term. While, buying, time, too, see, my, own, way, forward. Friends. Family. Authority. Where, was, the, loophole, is, what, I'm, asking.

"No." Is, an, interesting, monster. A, leading, excersise, in, why, hating, your, enemy, is, futile, when, you, can, always, in earnest, deny. Cheshire.

Vanity. Strong, sense, of, balance? I, suppose, as, long, as, a, strong, dosage, of, sanity, is, in, tow, it, just, might, create, a, brighter, indeed, after, all. Cheshire.

Shortly, into, the, official. I, decided, that, I, didn't, want, a, programmed, education. I, went, to, Howard, University, book, store. Barnes & Noble. Amazon.com. Had, several, conversations, with experience. Searched, and, found, that, freedom, employed, is, the, best, education. Enlightened, to know. T'is, the, only, program of recommendation, I, suggest, to those, able, to, master, themselves.

I, got, tired, of toning, my, judgment. So, I, stopped, judging. Agreeing to agree. Where I found, agreement. That, was my, vespon.

I, took, tap. Raised, on the beach, skate, path. And, have, perfectly, enlisted, Capoiera, Angola. Never, have I found a person, advanced, through their, lack, of effort.

I see, feel, and, know, that we, never, really, loose our, step. It's in the matter, of, remembering, the routine. There, is, truth, in the, old, adage. It, does, indeed, come, back, to you. It, does, indeed.

TO THE SURFACE.

◆

Romance. A theory, that, doesn't, equate to, my, current, sensories. Seems, a waste of time to process, in the wake of all, I'm, empiering. In, truth, t'is, the, prefer, that, I, reserve, such, process, for, the courting of, family. The mating of personal ambitions. Life, is, infinitely, more, fulfilling, and, leagues, more, abundant.

I, do, however, occasion, and, am, agreed, to, the, enlightenment, within, the, exchange, upon, understand, and, the, appreciation, for, acquaintance, amongst, time, without, amorous, affections. Indeed, a respect, and, care, I wouldn't, exchange, for, the, ecstasy, of them.

Pray, take, now. As, I, write, seated, upon, the, molded, walkway, defining, the, yarded, incline. Flanked, by, experienced, oaks. The, liberal, chartercourse, of, lentament. The, freedom, and, luxury, to contemplate, and, play, concept, to, the, day's, beauty. The, night's, enchantment.

Pray, on.

TO THE SURFACE.

◆

There, is, no, better, feeling, than, the, revelation, and, miracle, that, materializes, within, the, connectedness, of, one's, mental notes. Life, is, a, 3-D, prism. Careful.

There, is no, fuller, experience, than that, of the spiritual, and, cultural, pilgrimages, I have, had. Now, registered, into the, reestablishment, and, basic, warrant, and, substantiation, of, that, which, would, be, family, life.

I, think, of, the, study, of, Capoiera, Angola. An, African, form of, martial arts, survived, into, the, Americas. Passed, along, through, oral, physical, mental, teachings. Discipline, and, play.

The, two, roads, fuse, right, where, it, concerns, my, own, genetic, history. Contemporary, to the, thought: of, reacquainting, your, present, within, the, profound, reflection(s), of, who, you, are. Likened. Immediately, to, the, adoption, of, these, revelations, I, innuendo, the, rare, threads, that, uniquely, conjoin, even, the, prevailing, individualist. That, we, were, and, are, families, is, a, superlative, that, when, cognately, and, indubitably, applied, proves, infinitely, amazing. To, future, resources!

I, think, upon, my, paternal, grandfather. East Indian, born, within, the, West Indian, slave trade. Adopted, within, the, America's. Records, of, his, life, going, back, as, far as, Jamaica, only. Because, I've, met, him, only, once, at, age, 3, t'is, invaluable, for, me, to, device, the, details, that, would, provision. In, that, case, I, take it, upon, myself, to, absorb, all, that, applies. Made, available to me, within, that, part. So, that, I may, better, appreciate, my, affinity, within, this, kindred, I, understand, yet, hardly know.

And, so, it goes, with, all, of, my, branches.

My, native, Blackfoot. The, frill, of, my, European, lace. Complete, in, my, southern, rootage. Every, letter, every, pixel, fills, my, scope, on the world. My, purpose, within. Every, experience, a, new, order, of, color. As, life, becomes, activate, within, the, prism, that is my eye.

Availing, myself, to, the love, affair, that, is, Capoiera, Angola, I, therefore, am at, Zenith, with, this, world. There, is, nothing, more, calming, than, the, utter, capacity, of, this, life. Connecting, reenergizing, a, sensibility, of, long, ago. I, can, say, that, I've, never, experienced, so much, reverence, for, an, art, form. I, am, inspired, by, the, level, of, discipline, and, mastery. In, this, world, I, am, an, insatiable, perfectionist, with, spells, of, sprint. T'is, a, powerful, thing, winning, over, my, dedication, and, appreciation. T'is, a, basic, principle, of, being, respect. And, is, as, universal, as, it, appears.

As, a woman, to understand, the, rhythm, and, philosophy, of, combat, how, it, applies, to, the, relative, management, of, your, thought, and, function, within, the, everyday. These, perceptives, are, important. I, don't, know, anyone, who, reveres, want of making, a, best, decision, as, anything, less, than, wise.

There, are, days, I'd, much, rather, have, a, conversation, with, Orion, than, Venus. My, moon, centering, and, exiting, the stage. Than, to, be, unwinding, the, presupposed, stages, of, the, uncaptioned, two-minute, loss. The win is actually sweet. Yet, it's, win, to, win! This, theory, translates, throughout, any, design, or, lifetime. Indubitably.

This, time-aged, review, makes, all, the, difference, between, this, win, or, that, loss. Try. I, think, you'll, become, more, clear, on what it, is, I'm, speaking.

TO THE SURFACE.

◆

My, very, favorite, thing, to, do. Sight, and, accomplish.

More, so, people, than, any, other, thing. What, I, love, most, about, what, I, do. Entertainment. The, psychology, behind, the, "why." The basic, and, explicable, emanating, nature, of, a, thing. Reality, being: the, real, time, exchange, of, persons, to, environment, proves, far, more, fascinating, than, anything, we, could, ever, humor, you, with.

That, is, why, I, will, also, claim, travel. The, infinite, variable, of, people, to, experience.

Observation, relives, me, of, bias. Contributes, agreements, to, my, respectful, truth. Leaving, the, mundane, and, non-effective, behind. T'has, returned, my life, to, me, in, smooth, layers. And, in, wisdom, has, taught, leagues, more, than, the, superior, curriculum.

Preferably, the, human, form, at, its, best. The, animation. The, pure, unmeasured, expression. Force, equated, to, soul. It's, a, beautiful, thing.

From, the, common, to, the, elite. The, sensation, and, kind, that, find, expression, and, relevance, through, the, physical, form, translate, to, mechanical, and, theoretical, transmissions, that, bind. Case, in point: is, the, fascination, in dance. Though, bodies, in, motion, will, tend, to, stay, in, motion. No, two, will, ever, move, the, same. This, delicate, thesis, revels, a, vindicative, hybrid, of, thought. A, higher, context, of, encounter. The, free, will, of, a child, granted, permission, to, play. The, intense, focus, of, a, thinker, in, thought. Troubleshooter, upon, solution. The, magic, of, that, first, kiss. These, are, all, relevant, things.

These, days, I, find, connection, with, my, counter-gender. In, extension, to, physical, edification, I, find, a, satiate, in, the, witness, of, fellows, at, their, best. The, poise, and, confidence, of, someone, who, knows, what, their, doing. Otherwise, resourcing. Charm.

I, admire, respect. The, not, cowering, in, fear. Known. Fear: essentially, the, riddle, to, one's, quest, must, be, solved, while, holding, course, to, the, stave, of, courage's receipt. Convine, to, believe, no, other, navigation. For, those, without, confidence, will, not, lead, me.

Amen.

TO THE SURFACE.

Going, from, being, shaped, by, family, nucleus. To, being, shaped, and, formed, by, directors, photographers, journalists ,and, the, following, public. To, being, shaped, and, formed, by, otherwise, carriages. Caused, me, to, call, an, all, overdue, timeout.

My, spirit, expressed, in, the, alteration, of, all, that, my, reach, could, control. In, the, advertisement, of, my, self-proclaimed, new, era, I, make pronouncement, in, what, turns out, to, be, a, new, identity. This, distraction, that, worked, against, my, true, nature, and, advancement, was, under, strict, command, to, shell out. I, couldn't wait. Rather, looked, forward.

No, more, preoccupation, of, myself, with, others. With, "its", expression. No, more, tendrils. No, more, "at, length." Literally, I, myself, and, the, presence, of, a, wonderful, mind, would, move, on. Complete, and, void, of, all, attachments. T'was, upon, me, to, rise.

For, two-weeks, I, dreamt, of, this, surface. Finally, triumphing, in, my, efforts. To, succeed!

Finding, encouragement, and, cheer, within those, wise, enough, to, yen, the, yang. I, immediately, readied, progress. Insizing, new, display, I, afforded, myself, the, lesson. The, ignorance, of, conventional, intolerance. Never, wanting, for, self-definition, I, conclude, epiphany, to, research. I, also, learn, to, care, less, about, those, sinking, than, those, who, would, swim. Proceeding. Epitomy, of, free.

On, my, own. Free, of, illusion. Thankful, in, the, challenge, of, better, days. Also, having, the, time, that, belonged, to, all, that, care, now, mine! In, the, wake, of, these, stages, what, would, be, next?

Cheshire.

TO THE SURFACE.

Here's the crucst:

I, sincerely, remember, spending. Money, I, didn't, have. On, my, first, trip, to, the, Sundance, Film, Festival. What, a, whirl!

Freshly, separated. Living, with, a, friend. In, decision, with, which, direction, to, look, for, my, life, first.

Finally, between, writing, and, working, I, concur, that, introduction, of, myself, again, to, the, public, hastens, to, be, an, all, too, necessary, evil. As, facing, my, fears, head, on, one, by, one, or, heck, by, series, became the, paramount, issue, of, the, time. In, this, time, and, space, shy, would, have, to, go.

Getting about, acquainted, me, to, the, charm, and, education, not, to, mention, the, all, around, intelligence, begotten, by, variety. I, tell, you, that, fearless, socialization, advanced, my, "only, child" skills, by, worlds, and, eons. Quantums, and, isotopes. Play, by, glorious, play.

Firstly, and, most, importantly, asking, all, the, right, questions, learned, me, hope, to, successfully, produce, my, first, feature, film. Suddenly, "Get, it!" occurs, to me. By, daring, to, leap, into, the, nick, of, time, into, the, face, of, what, I want. My, eventuality, is, to, be, successful. So, with, eager, anticipation, I, willingly, gamble. Budget, to school, and, research.

Ah, for, the, hunt, of, new, ambition!

Absorbing, the, dynamic, for, conquest. Fueling, the, drive, for, inspiration. Taking off, at, ground, zero. Enjoying, the, art, of, the, build. This, blue, print, is, soon, realized. In, full. Because, I, want, it!

Cheshire!

TO THE SURFACE.

♦

(Sigh) Bridging, the, gap, of, highly, isolated, generations.

Grandfather, born, 1917. First, child, born, 1945. First, grandchild, born, 1973. A, great, one, born, 1999.

A, generation, of, world, war, and, great, depression. Of, loss, and, of, preservation. Of, compartmentalization, and, routine. An, opportunity, of, hierarchy, born. Well, guarded, by, a, system, of, cast, roles. Tradition. Giving, birth, to, Baby Boomers, New Agers, and, Revolutionists. Generations, who, began, to, realize, they, could, dream. Materialize. Effecting, sure, change, within, the, climate, of, their, socio-political, operatives.

This, sacrifice, forced a life, seen, for, or, through, the, enlisted, pioneers, of, Generation X. The, spoiled, and, entitled, who, built, upwards, from, a, world, of, repression, and, devastation. Distributers, of, this, new, identity. Where, defining, your, life, could, for, the, first, time, be, according, to, the, inspiration, of personal, design. Not, the, ordered, obligation, of, duty.

Untouched, by war. Addicted, to, immediacy. This, generation, advanced, in, its, affectation, to, convenience, and, technology. Making, a, swell, sophisticated, environment, from which, the, next, will, spring, forth, and, grow. Sprout, and, continue forth.

In this age, we have, gained, outwardly, yet, are neglected, inwardly. Might, seem to one, that, we, have, advanced, in all, of the, ways, that, don't, really, matter. These, as yet, unabridged, gaps, within, the, rapidly, advancing, highly, affected, age, testify, to this, all, too, clearly.

Polar, opposites, they are, in thought, and, attitude. It reflects. Clashing, belief, systems, all, aswirl, within a, rapidly, changing, system, of things.

Of, this, education, and, adaptation, will replace, assimilation.

Hallelujah!

Cheshire.

TO THE SURFACE.

In, an, age, where, many of, the, world's, contributors, are, women. Able, to, achieve, their, own, ambitions. Postponing, plans, for, family, in, order, to, amass, their, own, fortunes. In, an, age, where, they, no, longer, patrol, on, display, hoping, to be, plucked, by some, worthy, suitor. I, bid, you, Hallelujah!

In, an, age, where, well, planned, industries, combined, within, the, reach, and, speed, of, this, highly, technological, communicative, resource, called, cyberspace. Making, millionaires, out of the, average, fourteen-year, old, kid, in, record, timing, is as effortless, and, plentiful, as, the, very, ideas, they spew. The, shift of, power, fascinating. What, will, come, of, this, experiment?

In, this, age, I, determined, very, early, to, never, allow, myself, to, be limited, in choice, or, option. I, found, that, education, to, be, my, way, into, through, and, around, everything.

In, an, age, where, I have, observed, so, many, enslaved, to, and, not, with. In, an, age, where, I, have, dared, to wonder, why, a woman, is. In, an, age, that, promotes, the, fight. I, vow, never, to give up. Ever! Sealing, the, victory, within, the, twin, palms, of, one, cause!

In, an, age, where, emoticons, and, motivations, are, actively, and, freely, explored. Where, shining, symbols, wage, war, against, the, raging, insignia. I, victor.

In, an, age, no, longer, denied, yet, prescribed, I, tally, in, cue. Where, my, woman, dares, to, emerge, the, storm, courageous, undaunted, splendid, and, victorious. Again!

Cheshire.

WELCOME TO MY SOUL.

Are, we, not, all, natural, escapists? Does, not, imagination, make, that, so? Life's, dramatic, effects, suggest, the, assortment. We, play, the selection. Moving, one, in, pursuit, upon, realms, of, dignity, and, classique, halo.

Now, in, midst, upon, trialsome, trillows, are, amassed, files, of, wile, and, care. Centered, are, reloques, of, insight, and, imbue.

Sighting, for, the, wizard, I, am, intrigue, and, at, post. I'd, like, to think, I may, maintain, and, continue, upon, such, with, having, some, measure, of, fulfillment, and, challenge.

Precisely, I, have, mastered, the, art, of, make-believe. As, upon, the, world, of, a, child. Tomorrow, I, shall, pick-up, that, magic, stick, and, begin. Again.

THE RESOURCE.

I, remember. The, times, of, enrichment.

Nodding, in, thoughtful, agreement, with, teacher. Having, graduated, the, world, and, class, of, "babies." Heaven.

I, recollect, the, empowerment, that, came, upon, introduce, to, the, flashes, of, knowledge. The, very, prepared, revelations. I'd, made it!

I, remember, learning, after, the, winter, rains, that, the, mosquito, spawned, in, water. We, had, plenty, of it. For, there, were, plenty, of, storms, that, year, far, away, from, home, in, the, land, of, the, big kids.

Teacher, showed, us, how, to, stop, them, from, becoming, mature, blood-suckers. By, scooping, them, out. Drying, them, out. Yet, before, our, militia, could, master, the, skill, of, look, see, and, do, it, it, began, to hail. We, scrambled, inside, and, squealed, in, fascination. Watching, as, the, hard-packed, flakes, descended, in, sheets, and, piles.

My, eyes, dart, in the direction, of, the, blue, upon, white, row, boat, in, our, land, of, ground, and, play. Location, of, mosquitoed, enemy. Scoping, the, texture, of, the, slushy, surface, I, was, affirmed. T'was, a, war, of, the, worlds, and, I, had, box, seats.

Stooping, at, the, picture, window, you, could, see, the, bobbing, and, rippling, of, the, clumsy, ice berg, miniatures. The heavens, maintaining, their, steady, attack.

I, tell, you, between, the, armaric, force, of, us, big, kids, and, this, unexpected, act, from, God, those, pesky, mosquitoes, never, had, a, chance.

I, then, recall, my, comrade. Corn, fed, rosy, cheeks, bright, eyes, hair, and, smile. A pure, presence, that, called, to, your, attention. I, didn't, forget. "Hi. I'm, Julliette." She, sings, out, in, stacattoed, bubbles. I flash, my, moment, away, in, order, to, greet. From, my, intense, construction, of, blocks, before, the, window. "Hi." I smile, as, I, scan, her, for, purpose. "What's, your, name?" Bloop. Bloop. Bloop! "Lark." I report, matter of factly, as, I, take, her, in. "I, live, across, the, street. Where, do, you live?" She, continued. "A, little, ways, further." I confirm. "Can, I, play?" She, invited. Transferring, from, standing, to sitting, position, to, help, me build.

In, a world, misinformed, upon, opinion, t'is, requite, upon, these, mass, acompassed, runs, esque, to, reinventment, and, relatives. As, on a, first, day, in, kindergarten, 'pon, invention, of, the, sematics. Dirge, the, benefits. Cause, the reconciliation. Fright the scabe, upon, the, mighty, means of, nesposite.

Whether, teacher, to student. Begetting, friends, at, play. Authority, must, recompense, its, influence. Whether, yay, or, nay. This, is, the, fundamental, and, elementary, truth.

Amen.

THE RESOURCE.

I, remember, the, members, only, accelerate, reading, course, for, the, advanced, reader. I, remember, it, only, being, Juliette, and, I. That, everlasting, reality, of greatness.

I, remember, the, books, vivid, in illustration. Illustrious, in, meaning. To, my, surprise, glory, and, delight, T'was. She, in her chair, we, on, the, floor, legs, crossed, attention, rapt. Hindwhile, necessities, capped, our, peak. I, remember, the, difference. I, remember, the, importance. I, remember, never, wanting, it, to, change.

I, remember, sitting, at the table, for, concentration. The, sheer, excitement. Being, graced, by, instruction. "Choose, all, activities, appealing, to you." She, instructed. As, it, was, International Day. "Select, clearly, from, everything, you would, like, to learn." She, furthered. Courses, in cuisine. Sessions, in, music. Advanced, art & sport. I, would, finally, explore, beyond, kindergarten, square. Introduce, of, the, higher, learned, had, my, mind, abright. Operation: Global Explore, on, the, horizon. To, command, and, conquer: the, ultimate, theme.

To, dream: I would, indeed, negotiate, to, investigate, beyond, this, extrenuating, waiting, period. With, a, two-week, target, on, the, making, I, was, indeed, going, to, have, to, morale, the, span, of, things. For, sure, t'would, be, a, mastular, upulture, of, indignant, proportions. Scores, beyond, the, construction, paper, flagging, in, my, right, hand. Colors. Woa.

THE RESOURCE.

◆

Finally, the, day, of, reckoning. Finally, to, absorb, the, prophesed, impact, upon, my mind. I, exalted, in the, exchange. Monday's, news, would, reap. The, glory, in, that, reteal. My, the, halo, repute! The, long, awaited, for, commemorate, had, arrived!

I, keep, time. Finding, my, eyes, and, mouth, to, be, agape, as, I, take in, this, massive, construct, and, well, planned, layout, of, asphalt, beautifully, groomed, grounds, and, entire world, of bi-level, playland. Space Odyssey 2000, begins, to, ring in my ear.

In, liberation, from, that, ocular, space, I, am, indeed, in, case, with, fever, and, heightened, in, intent. Enthused, to, be, aparty, to the elite.

In, the, days, awakening, one, has, but, to, perceive, the, monumental, consorts, that, epitomize, the, elemental. Upon, concept, t'is, the, expectate, to, realize, procurement. In, the tender, stage, of, engender, t'is, wise, to, proclamate, to plan. The, wealth, of, balance, inspires, one, to intruse.

Now, there, is, real, value, in, statements, of, pure, rare, measure. Faculties, comparted, to realms of institution. So, much, so, that, in, the, wake, of, congenial, efforts, one, must, wake, with, a start. With, a, destine, to, rise.

That, been, said. Having, completed, the, Pavlov, circuit. My, final, destination, is, The Bowl. The Bowl: the, biggest, park, I've, ever seen. Something, of, the, size, of, a, massive, crater, housing, all, if, not, most, of, the, world's, relative, tools, for, play. Important, where, you, measure, one's, means, of, proficient, affluence. Where, the, criteria, for, essential, necessity, does, class, and, contrast, the, leading. T''is, here, at: The Bowl: where, I would, learn, to play soccer (hunt, down, catch, and, blast, the, life, out, of, this, ball).

Tineswhile, I, collapse, onto, the, field. In, breathless, epiphany. Peering, up, into, the, bight, sky, I, take, notice, of, the, pastel, wedge, that, whispers, across, its, vast, clarity. In, truth, this...is, to, be, absolute, rhapsody.

I, go, back, as, often, as, I, can.

ART & LITERATURE.

◆

In, all, the, history, of, the, world. There, has, never, been, a, majoring, tally, of, the, bind, like that of, music. I've, heard, music, so, exquisite, I, could, feel, the, hues. I've, heard, music, so divine, I, transcended, upon, the, invisible.

The, world, of, syncomphrancy. Its ability to, charm, the, sourest, of notes. To elate, and, inspire, the most, complex, of orders. Its, influence, predates, even, written, language. The, ability, to, communicate, the, intimate, the, abroad. Transfix, whole, worlds, upon, compose. The, basis, within, this, division, of, recorded, legacy, lies, in, its, infuse, ability, to, enchant, and, carry. The, all, known, comportment, of, its, savoir, and, power, onto, enlightenment, has, both, marveled, and, transformed, the whole, of, time, and, times, from the, very, genesis, of the, world.

Such, an, influence. One, could, suppose, to, be, of, monument, and, of, mammothed, proportions. Ties, of, leagues, raised, incendiaries, caps, of, height, all, unison, at, its, charge. Time, has, proven, not, the, better, without, it. And, the, muse, still, holds, her, card.

This, secret, world, transfixed, upon, unions, of, compart, shall, ever, exist, one, of, dearest, value.

Now, in, raise, of, heaven, an, accompaniment, to the, earth, shall we, more, give, or, for, that, matter, gain, light, in, relevance, to, the, higher, markations, of, express, upon, elevate. The, unencumbered, chamber, of, thought, on, code, within, divine, recordings, of, record, on, insight. Leafs, of, tale, and, time, ought, not, soon, deny, portrayal, fancied, upon, epitome's peak. Where, remembrance, accelerates, accustomed, acquaintance, and, and, greets, upon, minueted, grace.

Enter, textile's, harmoquin. Where, worlds of class, explain. Liquid, visions, adance, the, rare, seen, flight. And, harmony's, dreams, ignite, the, phoenix, in, stroke, of, midnight. Where, nuance, encadences, measure, of, brightest, ingrite. Where, brilliance, thickens, the, exist, to, fight.

I, am, membered.

Thank, you.